Bike Packing 202

A Complete Guide

Everything You Should Have Learned
in 101 and a Lot More

William R. Lamb

Cover image © William R. Lamb

www.innovativeinkpublishing.com
Send all inquiries to:
4050 Westmark Drive
Dubuque, IA 52004-1840

ISBN: 9-798-7657-4068-2

Published in the United States of America

Bike Packing 202

Everything You Should Have Leaned in 101 and a lot More

Contents

Chapter 1

What Is Bike Packing

If someone would've told me that riding a bike packed with a few of my belongings in the middle of nowhere would change my life forever, I would've said they really didn't know me very well. After doing so, I found that I was the one who didn't know me very well. It's hard to explain the good one gets from occasionally leaving the concrete jungles behind. Spending time in nature is one of the best ways to rejuvenate one's soul. Slowly, your senses awaken, and a feeling of being free starts to breathe deep inside you. Your needs begin to simplify, as do your desires. You become overwhelmed by emotions, and then you become still. And for many, for the first time in a long time, you meet "you".

I return from every bike packing adventure with one regret, that I can't share all that I felt and saw with the rest of the world. The lens of a camera captures but a still image, a moment in time, and yet that image can overwhelm when it's viewed upon by the human eye. The eye doesn't simply see but also allows the brain to imagine what it felt like to be in that moment. Simply put, a photograph doesn't come close to allowing the viewer to feel what it feels like to be a part of that moment.

Outside of our self-made jungles there exists a world full of unblemished beauty in forms that are simply unimaginable just waiting to free every emotion we possess. It's an adventure that is unique for each person who chooses to take it. Rarely does a day pass without my mind finding its way back to a place along the trail. Those feelings remind me to breathe, to put things back in perspective, and to be thankful for the places outside the jungle that wait patiently for my return. At times they feel distant and as if but a dream, a dream that's only a bike ride away.

Bike packing is basically a combination of biking and camping with a little hiking thrown in. Trips can vary from as short as overnight to as long as several weeks; they can be weekend getaways by yourself or with a group of friends and everything in between. Most of all, bike packing is inexpensive after the initial cost of purchasing equipment. The US is full of state and national parks to ride in, and many—in fact, most— are free to camp in as well. There are an infinite number of areas to ride, and if you don't like camping, you can plan your route so that day's end will find you in a town with lodging services. The Race Across Texas, which many view as a ride, developed by race director Kevin Lee, is a great example of the different ways one can begin bike packing. The race starts in Texarkana, Arkansas, and ends in Tucumcari, New Mexico (1,029 miles), and consists of mostly the gravel back roads of Texas. The route was developed to allow you to camp along the way, or lodge—the choice is yours. The race/ride has a supported category and a non-supported category. *Supported category* means that someone carries what you need and provides support along the route. *Non-supported* means you are on your own and responsible for yourself. Perhaps a mixture of the two may be the right way for some. Because the route has so many waypoints, you may begin or end your ride in a number of different places, meaning the length of the ride can be easily adjusted to fit your needs. The route is relatively tame in terms of terrain, unless of course the weather turns bad; however, there are plenty of alternate routes if needed. It's really a great race for those who want to test their skills in an area where help is readily available as opposed to their first long journey in more remote country.

When doing the Tour Divide from Canada to Mexico, I mostly camped, but in the last Race Across Texas I lodged all six nights. There are companies, such as Adventures by Bike, that will help plan your trip, provide equipment, provide education in the form of camps or clinics. and have a guide accompany you along the way. The positives are many, and the negatives are few.

As I said earlier, never in my wildest dreams would I have believed bike packing would have had such a profound influence on me as it has. It has changed the way I approach so many things in my everyday life. After the Tour Divide, I was asked to speak to several organizations for a variety of reasons about my experiences and what I had taken away from it. Below is a summary of what I learned from a simple 3,000-mile trek across the United States.

After the Tour Divide in 2016 I came to the realization that we as individuals are awesome and capable of so much more than we think. When faced with adversity, all too often we convince ourselves that quitting is the right thing to do. Quitting is never the right thing to do. There are multiple paths to success, but each path starts with you accepting that as truth. Yes, some ways are much easier than others, but the tough paths are usually the ones that we learn the most from and the ones that tend to shape who we are and who we are to become. Excuses are just part of the brain's way of helping us to avoid pain. Pain is simply weakness leaving the body. We must change our mindset to one which says we will succeed despite our perceived limitations and that we all, though individually different in many ways, are born with all the tools we need. It's the mind not the body that determines our success. Did I want to quit? Yes, many times. Was there ever a good reason to quit? Yes, many times, but there was always a better reason to finish. The inner battles that we face will always be there, but right alongside them is the inner strength that too will always be there. Never be afraid to fail. Trying and failing is always better that accepting defeat without a fight. It's great to have a plan, it's great to have help, it's great to have unlimited resources, and it's even greater the moment you realize you have always possessed all three. Pursue whatever you do with a passion, be significant, and believe in yourselves. There are many times when lesser athletes win the battle, a lot of David and Goliath stories, and it's okay to be David. He is Lord

Chapter 2

How to get Started

Once you decide that you might like to give bike packing a try, you should start by taking a short overnight or weekend trip with someone who has adequate experience in bike packing. Adventuresbybike.com, for example, is a company that can help you plan and complete a trip without buying all the equipment. They provide everything, and if you enjoy it, they can point you in the right direction. You can also check with local bike shops for recommendations as to whom you could trust to take you out for the first time. When you feel you are ready to venture out on your own, make the first couple of adventures overnight or weekend adventures in an area you are familiar with and, if possible, in mild conditions. It doesn't matter how much you have read, viewed, or prepared in general; you can expect it to be quite different when you are by yourself for the first time.

As you grow in confidence and experience, you'll find yourself eager to go on a much longer adventure. I still believe you should do so with at least one other person if not a group, especially if your destination is in the remote wilderness. Don't get me wrong, I think everyone should do something in their life where they have no one to depend on but themselves; a lot can be learned about oneself when doing so. However, safety is the most important thing, and you are much safer the more experience you have. The old saying hurry up and wait comes to mind. Make sure when you feel you are ready that you actually are, and even then, understand it will most likely not go as planned.

With proper planning, bike packing can be a safe and very enjoyable way to spend some time decompressing and enjoying the endless beauty our world has to offer. It can serve as some great times among good friends and even a great way to make new ones. The following chapters will get you started the right way.

If you are not a skilled mechanic, taking a course in bike repair and learning as much as you can about repairing your own bike is of extreme importance. You do not necessarily have to become the world's greatest mechanic, but you must be able to

- Perform tire and wheel repair:
    - Be able to repair a tire, whether its patching or replacing a tube, repairing a tire casing that's been cut or damaged, or plugging a tubeless tire.
    - Be able to remove and reinstall a front or back wheel properly to be able to repair a tire.
    - Be able to remove a tire from a wheel and replace it properly.
    - Be able to remove and replace a valve stem properly.
    - Be able to remove and replace a spoke.
    - Be able to straighten an alloy wheel that's been bent to a ridable wheel.

- Perform repairs on the drivetrain:
  - Be able to maintain and or repair a broken or bent chain.
  - Be able to replace a derailleur hanger.
  - Be able to replace a broken or frayed derailleur cable.
  - Be able to adjust cables to both derailleurs if necessary.
- Perform repairs and adjustments to the brakes:
  - Be able to maintain and or replace brake pads.
  - Be able to replace a broken or frayed brake cable.
  - Be familiar with the operation of hydraulic brakes and how to adjust them.
- Perform general adjustments:
  - Be able to adjust seat and handlebar positions.
  - Be able to adjust the headset.
  - Be familiar with how your devices are mounted and how to adjust those mounts.
  - Be familiar with the cleats on your shoes and how to maintain and replace them.
- Perform routine maintenance:
  - It is important to properly maintain your bike, especially during an adventure. Keeping the drivetrain and chain clean and lubed, the derailleurs and brakes properly adjusted, and maintaining proper tire pressure all go a long way in increasing your odds of having fewer problems.

I would practice each of the above skills several times until you build the confidence in your ability to comfortably perform them. With confidence in your ability to repair most of the problems you may experience with your bike will come a certain sense of peace when you are alone in the great outdoors. Obviously, to make the repairs you must have the proper tools with you, and those tools are dependent on the bike setup. Chapter 8 contains a list of the tools I carry, and you can see how it differs between the bikes that I use.

Chapter 3

Choosing the right Bike

Choosing the right bike is the first step to insuring a good experience once you have decided bike packing is for you. There are mainly three options available: full suspension, hardtail, and fully rigid. Each one has certain benefits that are suited to particular terrains, and if you could own all three that would be great. Since most can only own one, I'll give you an overview of each and then give you my recommendation.

A full suspension bike provides more comfort on rough terrain that is continual, assuming you could stay in the saddle of course, and on long stretches of gravel roads filled with washboard. It also requires fewer bike skills to navigate those terrains than do the other two. For the bike packer who prefers shorter distances and doesn't ride a lot at race pace, it's not a bad choice. If longer distances at a faster pace is your choice, it's not the bike for you. Longer distances with fewer waypoints require one to carry more supplies. The rear shock takes up lots of room and requires you to have a smaller frame bag, and the front shock doesn't serve as a good place to mount water bottles. The shocks also require the handle bar bags, as well as the seat bags, to be kept small so that when they compress the bags won't touch and rub the tires. A full suspension bike is heavier and harder to carry in areas where you may be required to hike your bike, and it has more components—thus, more can go wrong. In general, if it's a rough, rocky climb, one tends to be out of the saddle, and on rough downhills one is always out of the saddle. Lots of energy waste as well when the shocks are utilized, so one is locking and unlocking shocks a lot. All in all, it's great for short trips with plenty of waypoints on rough terrain.

A hard tail is much more efficient, especially when climbing, it **weighs less** due to no rear shock, and on flatter sections it's quicker. It provides more area for a larger frame bag as well as a larger seat bag, thus allowing for more supplies. As mentioned above, the rear shock isn't utilized as much as one would think. The one disadvantage would be gravel roads with long, flat stretches of washboard. On long rides however, more supplies are a good trade-off. All in all, the pros outweigh the cons. It's not only the better choice for most, but it also costs less.

The third option is the fully rigid, which has widely been the choice of most professional, hard-core bike packers and endurance racers. The fully rigid has no suspension whatsoever and therefore is a bit less smooth than the previous two types mentioned. It does, however, have several advantages, such as less weight and fewer parts to have problems with, and it is by far the most suitable for carrying a full range of supplies. There is room for both a large seat bag as well as a large handle bar roll. It also has room for a larger frame bag as well as the ability to mount cages on the front fork to carry extra water and supplies. It does require a bit more skill in technical sections, but generally one is not bombing down those type of sections with a fully loaded bike. For what it's worth, it's the bike of choice for me, although I have made a few modifications, which we will discuss later in the chapter.

Once you have chosen a style of bike, it's now time to choose the material the bike is constructed from as well as the components it will be outfitted with. Material choices are steel, titanium, or carbon. Steel is rugged and dependable but heavy, titanium is lighter and softer but more expensive, and carbon is the lightest and generally the most expensive. As with everything, when it comes to bikes, there are pros and cons to all three. Steel frames that consist of higher grade steels are the most dependable and easiest to repair, as well as the cheapest to buy. They must be painted, or they will rust. Titanium is next when it comes to dependability. They don't require paint, they rival carbon frames when it comes to weight and rigidity, and their ride quality is exceptional. Since titanium is less widely available than steel, they are quite a bit more expensive than steel, and due to their resilience, it's harder to find someone to weld them if they break or crack. Carbon is the lightest and the most expensive. Although it can be as stiff as the others and very durable, it is way more susceptible to damage. The top tube, for example, will not dent like steel or titanium when hit with a blunt object; it will crack. During a fall, a rock or a stump can be just as effective as a hammer in rendering your bike useless. The choice is yours, and again, for what it's worth, I prefer a good quality steel frame. For sponsor reasons, I did do the Tour Divide on a Salsa Cutthroat with a carbon frame.

A quick note on suspension: in general, I (as do most) prefer a fully rigid bike for adventure racing. There is a fork on the market, however, that I have started using, and it is outstanding. The Lauf Fork, which never needs servicing and has no moving parts, is virtually indestructible and has just enough travel to make short work of washboard and provides a ton of relief on your hands during long multiple-day rides. It still provides the rigidity necessary to allow you to carry a handle bar roll and is the choice I now use on all my endurance bikes. Check it out at Laufcycles.com.

Also, I use a belt drive system made by Gates that works great. My bike of choice is a SPOT Brand Rocker single speed. No one does a better bike/belt drive combination than SPOT and Gates. The performance is unparalleled and its maintenance-free. I have no need to carry chain lubes, brushes, or links, thus saving me weight and room. I have about 17,000 miles on the belt, and it's still good to go. They make a hub with internal gears that allows for a belt drive as well. Why do I ride a single speed? Scan the QR code and find out. ☺

Chapter 4

Bike Setup

Once you have settled on a bike, the next step is to have it set up to fit you properly. If the bike is not setup properly it could result in injuries that could shorten your journey. Knee and Achilles strains, hands and feet numbness, irritation to the bum, as well as back and neck pain are just some of the symptoms that may arise from an improperly fit bike. After being fit, many hours should be spent on the bike to dial in the fitting even more. In general, setting the bike up in more of a touring position is the most comfortable. Many choose to set the bike up as if they were racing, which puts one in a more aggressive position and greatly reduces comfort, only to find after a day or two that they are actually slower due to fatigue.

I have found that setting the handlebars equal to or higher than the seat height greatly reduces hand and back discomfort both during and after the journey. **Wearing shoes that are at least a size and a half larger than normal allows room for the feet to swell (which they will on long rides), thus reducing foot pain.** It also allows more room for wearing waterproof socks, which are generally thicker, when needed. Having multiple places to grip the bars can also reduce hand and neck pain.

Areas where you touch the bike are prone to be the most troublesome for everyone so special care should be put into how the feet, bum, and hands attach or rest. Avoid falling into a trap where you simply set up your bike the way you have read that others do. Information from those of us who have put in countless hours on a bike is valuable and should serve as a good starting point, but in the end, the bike must be comfortable to you not me. As with most everything, individuals have different preferences, and what works for one may not work for another. Once the bike is dialed in, record everything so that if parts need to be replaced along the way it will be easy to put them back in the right position. Close doesn't work; increments of as little as half a centimeter can make a huge difference.

Remember, getting fit is just a starting point. Continue putting in hours while dialing in the fit, and in the long run it will be well worth the effort.

Chapter 5

Choosing the Right Components for the Bike

Your next goal should be to equip your bike with the most reliable components that you can and do so as affordably as you can. Fortunately for you, the most reliable components are sometimes the least expensive. The weight of a component often determines the price: the lighter, the more expensive. One must remember, however, expensive doesn't always mean reliable.

First, let's look at drive trains. The choices are basically 3X, 2X, or 1X. In other words, you can have as many as 3 chain rings on the front or as little as 1. A 3X weighs more but generally provides a wider range of highs and lows. A 2X drops a bit of weight but also narrows the range of highs to lows, and a 1X weighs the least and up until recently offered the smallest range of highs to lows available. What you are looking for is one or two easy gears you can climb the steep climbs with and one or two gears you can use to really make short work of the flat sections. In my opinion, the triple has too much redundancy and offers little benefit over the 2X, especially with the rear cassettes that are offered today. Due to new technology, I think the 1X or single chain ring on the front is the best bet. Both Sram and Shimano now have 1x12 drive trains with a cassette that ranges from ten to fifty-two teeth cogs, with a wide variety of tooth counts available on the front chain ring as well. This is much more reliable and allows you to have only one shifter and derailleur as opposed to two of each. Less weight and less things to go wrong. I use a Chris King bottom bracket because they are an industry leader in their components and have been for years and they are easily serviceable. I also still use Carbon cranks. I have from the beginning and have never had an issue with any. They are lighter and reasonable in price. All in all, the choice is yours, but for what it's worth, I use a 1X1—in other words, a single speed. ☺

Next comes the brakes. Again, there are several choices. You can go with caliber or disc, with hydraulic or cables. Really, with today's technology the choice is mostly hydraulic or cables because disc is the most reliable and certainly the most widely used. Choosing between hydraulic and cables depends on what you are most comfortable with. Hydraulics are more expensive than cables, but cables are more reliable. Cables can be easily replaced on the trail; hydraulics are not easy to repair on the trail at all. They do make hydraulic calibers that are cable actuated, and that's what I chose on the divide, but I had very little success with them. All in all, I think hydraulic is the best way to go. If you were to fall during a ride and break a brake line, it's very unlikely you would break both, so you would still have at least one functioning brake to get you to a place where it could be repaired.

Wheels and tires come next. There are so many good wheels out there to choose from. Carbon or alloy—it's all about weight and money. It's the same old story that carbon is lighter and costs more; alloy is heavier but more dependable and costs less. Carbon wheels today are so durable it's not funny, and they truly rival alloy in dependability to some extent. I have bent aluminum wheels during a ride and was able to beat them back in shape enough to still ride the bike, but if you crack a carbon wheel you are on foot. In my opinion it's not always about weight; it's about a beginning and an end and your ability to get there safely. Your bike plays an important role in you doing so. I use Chris King hubs on the rear for three reasons: they are dependable, rebuildable, and Chris King has been an industry leader for a long time. I view wheels and tires differently than most in that I want them to be the most reliable regardless of weight. I run tubeless wheels and tires; it's the only way to go. To insure they are leak-free, I use two full wraps of tape on each wheel and 4-6 ounces of orange seal in each tire. I also use Teravail Sparwood tires with heavy side walls. This is a much heavier combination than most would use. In the last three years, however, I have had zero flats. I've done the Tour Divide (3,000 miles) followed by the Race Across Texas (1,029 miles) on the same set of tires, no flats. In my opinion go with Stan's no-tube wheels, Chris King hubs, and Teravail tires filled with orange seal, and you're good. Wayne's Precision Wheels builds all my wheels. He's the best because that's all he does. His contact info as well as the contact info of all the products I use are listed in the back of the book.

Handlebars and seat posts are available in carbon, titanium, and alloy. The same holds true for the pros and cons as the above products—lighter costs more. I use titanium for both the seat post and the handlebars just because of the weight they must support with the bags that are attached to them. Titanium is tough yet light, so it's a no-brainer.

Saddles are the most important piece of equipment you'll ever purchase. I personally have tried them all, and not until this last one did I experience a long ride without serious pain every day. The bottom line is that getting fit is a start but not a fix-all. I am always at a loss when a fitter asks me how it feels after ten minutes. They all feel fine after ten minutes, but what I'm concerned with is how they feel after twenty straight hours a day several days in a row. Getting fit is a good starting point if you will follow that with several long days on the bike in a row, and even that's not a sure thing. It's the same with saddles as with everything, according to most people, every ounce counts. Again, I disagree. I found my saddle with the help of a guy I rode with for a while on the Divide, Hal Russell. Hal told me to get a Brooks B17 and be done with it, and he was right. The saddle breaks in to fit your bum after about 300 to 400 miles, and you're done. My last 1,029-mile race across Texas on a rigid single-speed was pain-free for the first time since picking up the sport. The saddle is old school, a rail on each side and across the back that hold the leather cover suspended above them, it's like sitting in a swing and it works. Yes, it's heavier and harder to take care of, and no, it doesn't look as cool as others, but it's comfortable, and in the end that's all that matters. **The majority of those who start rides and quit before they reach their destination do so because of excruciating pain caused by the saddle.**

It's best to use quality equipment, and yes, lighter is better in some cases, but reliability is the key, especially since the majority of those bike packing are not racing. Bike packing is an awesome way to experience the outdoors. Remember, it's still the great outdoors, and nature sometimes can be harsh. Getting stuck in the middle of nowhere is mostly a lack of planning, and that planning starts with the equipment you have chosen to get you from here to there.

Chapter 6

The Gear

When it comes to the gear you use, it's a process that requires trial and error. There are so many products out there that all claim to be the best, and each piece may be the best for someone because they have never tried anything else. I have tried a lot of different products and have settled on the ones that have served me well and are priced appropriately.

Let's start with **the bags** we use to carry our necessities on the bike. Everything we need to survive must be stored in those bags, so it's imperative that they do their job. What needs to stay dry must stay dry, what needs to stay cold must stay cold, and so forth. Your well-being depends on it. I settled on two brands, **Revelate Designs** and **Bike Bag Dude**. Revelate Designs makes the best seat bag (the terrapin system) bar none, and Bike Bag Dude makes the best most custom fit frame bags in the world. Both companies are very dependable and well respected. Revelate Designs doesn't make custom frame bags specifically for your bike, and the ones they do make that I've used in the past tend not be waterproof like their seat bags are. The ones made for me by Bike Bag Dude are made specifically for my bike and are extremely durable as well as waterproof. The bags I use are as

follows: Revelate Designs seat bag, Yakataga Dry Pocket handlebar bag, Jerrycan top tube bag, Bike Bag Dudes Frame bag, Gas tank top tube bag, handlebar roll, and two Chaff bags on the handlebars.

The **lighting system** is the next thing one needs to sort out. When I first started riding at night I used battery powered lights, and it didn't take me long to realize there were some major disadvantages to doing so. First and foremost, the need to replace batteries. Rechargeable batteries were no good because they had to be recharged somewhere, so basically you had to carry an endless supply of batteries. I raced the Stagecoach 400 and my first race across Texas that way, and it was doable because of the endless number of towns within 40 or 50 miles of each other where you

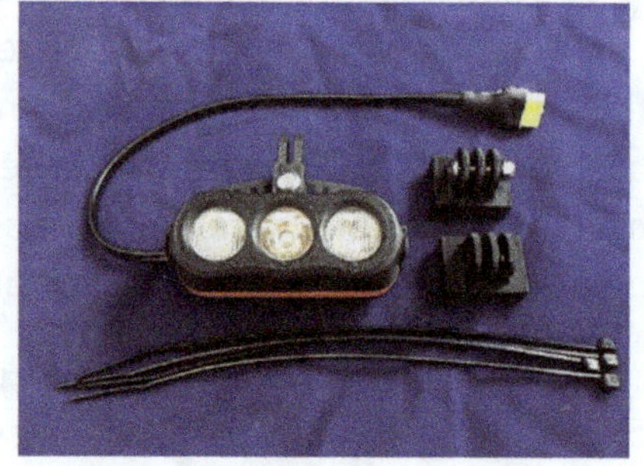

could buy batteries if needed. I never felt like I could get off the grid when batteries were my source of power. Then I found K-Lite and the Son dyno-hub and never looked back. The K-Lite is the best on the market, and its creator, Kerry Staite, is a genius. He works endlessly to improve his invention and has made it virtually indestructible. With the use of a pass-through battery my hub keeps my Garmin and phone charged all day and runs my lights at night, which allows me to never have to plug in for anything. I am aware there is always a chance that the hub could malfunction, and so for that reason I carry an Aye-Up light and battery for emergencies, but in three years I have never had to use it. The K-Lite at night stays on after I stop for about 20 minutes, which gives me plenty of light to set up camp. I also carry a couple of Stix USB LED lights to use around camp. They are the size of about half a stick of gum and weigh nothing. I charge them every 3 or 4 days using the pass-through battery, which is always full due to the dyno-hub's endless source of energy. There's no reason to look any further; this is the only way to light your ride properly.

Navigation is next on the list since knowing where you are being of utmost importance. I use a Garmin 1030—actually, I have two of them for redundancy. Both are loaded with the same routes. I use the Garmin 1030 because it plugs right into my pass-through battery and never requires charging. Again, the hub could fail, and the backup Garmin is there the same as the Aye-Up light, just for emergencies. I also have the routes downloaded to my Ride with GPS, so they are accessible with my phone and a printed town list with the distance to each town printed beside it.  When maps are available of the route I highly recommend carrying them. This is another area where weight is not as important as safety. Being lost in the great outdoors could prove to be a mistake you may not overcome. Many of my friends use the Garmin Etrex for navigation and have great success with it. Just remember the Etrex require batteries, and if that is your choice make sure you carry more than you think you might need. You should carry a second unit as well.

Hand comfort is always an issue, and the best way to deal with it is to have several places for your hands to hang out while you are riding. For me, part of the answer was the Bar Yak—crazy name for sure, but it works. This piece of equipment not only gave me better options for mounting my lights and Navigation device, but it also provided two extra places to place my hands while riding. Multiple hand positions help to relieve pressure being applied to a single place in the hands, thus helping to avoid the long-term numbness that follows. On extremely long races everyone experiences some hand discomfort afterwards but having multiple places to hang on can greatly reduce that. After my last race my hands stayed numb for about four months. This was a much

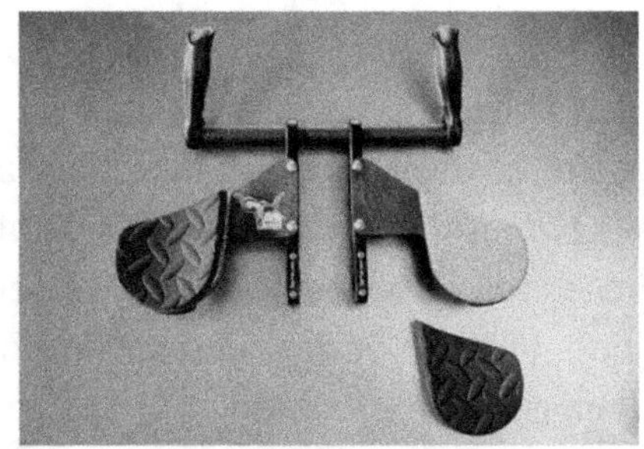

shorter race than the Tour Divide, only seven days on the bike. The thing about bike packing is that you are always learning, and this was a good learning experience for me. It was the first time I had raced with flat bars and yes, the bike was equipped with a Bar Yak. The rest of the setup was quite different, however. I had always raced my long races on my Salsa Cutthroat, and before that my Salsa Fargo, both with drop bars and both with the bars set higher in more of a touring position. My Spot Rocker was my single-speed set up for racing in the trails as well as short 200 mile or less marathon-type races. The handlebars were set much lower in a racing position, which put me much more on top of them. It was equipped with a Lauf fork, the same as on my Cutthroat, and I decided not to replace the fork with a new Lauf that I could cut in a way that would allow me to set it up like a touring bike. After all, the race was only 1,029 miles and tame when it came to the terrain I would be riding on. Turns out that was a bad idea, but that bad idea helped me better understand the physics of different bike setups. My new rule is when riding multiple days in a row and being on the bike more than sixteen hours a day, one should always have the bars above or equal to their saddle height period.

Hydration is also key when riding in the great outdoors. There are many ways to carry water, and it comes down to which is best for the individual. Your options include hydration packs that you wear on your back like Camelbacks, water bottles you carry on your bike, and even water bladders you can carry in your frame bag. Most use a combination of the three. I use bottles on the bike and carry a bladder that I can use on long stretches where I might not be able to refill. There are a couple things to take note of when it comes to water: **you can never have too much**, and it's hard to drink when it's extremely hot (the water that is, not the air temperature). One can survive without food much longer than they can without water, so always carry enough. I use Bike Bag Dude Chaff bags to carry two insulated 24 oz bottles on my handlebars; this keeps the water cool much longer than you would think. I also carry two 24 oz insulated bottles on my frame. The insulated bottles are heavy but do keep the water cooler than regular bottles. I utilize the frame bottles first, since they cannot keep the water as cool as the bottles in the Chaff bags, and then move to the handlebar bottles. I always carry a 4-liter bladder folded in my  frame bag in case I reach a stretch where I am uncomfortable with my supply options—always better to be safe than sorry. I never use a hydration pack on my back; it tends to make my neck hurt. Sometimes I'm on my bike for up to 20 hours a day, and that takes enough of a toll on my back. ☺

Clothing plays more of a role than one thinks. Choosing what to wear daily and what to have handy if needed takes some trial and error as well as a little planning. At the top of the list are shoes. It's best to wear your shoes one and a half sizes too big, which allows room for the feet to swell without the shoes becoming too tight. It also allows room to move the feet around when hot spots arise after a long day on the bike. Choosing to wear bib shorts or regular bike shorts is a personal preference. The cleats you use are also very much up to what the individual has grown accustomed to. I use SPDs because they are simple to connect and disconnect from the pedals. They are a bit apt to pick up rocks and mud but it's what I've used ever since I began riding, and there is just a certain comfort to them.

You may find bike shorts are more practical since they do not require you to remove your top to use the restroom and such. I personally like bib shorts because they seem to hold their position while riding better and are not as apt to rub. I always wear a bike jersey with pockets on the back for extra storage if needed, and the material works well when it's hot or cold. I never wear gloves unless it's cold. I have relatively dark skin and don't seem to burn easily. If it's so hot that my hands get sweaty, I wear a very thin full-fingered glove. If I feel the weather may turn I carry my Showers Pass Crosspoint glove in a back pocket on my jersey. The gloves are extremely lightweight as well as windproof and waterproof. Half-fingered gloves tend to irritate the areas between the fingers and sometimes reduce blood flow to the fingers. When it comes to socks I recommend Defeet Woolie Boolie. They are made of merino wool, remain odorless for a long period of time, and can be worn multiple days without laundering. I carry a short and a long pair when weather is questionable. Lightweight cycling caps provide protection from sweat getting in the eyes and also allow less damage to the hair from the helmet moving around. A bandana is always a must, especially when dusty conditions are possible—and they are always possible on gravel and dirt. It's good to have a lightweight Endura Pakajak in case of wind and rain. The jackets are wind- and water-resistant and fold up to the size of a small wallet. I store mine in one of the pockets on the back of my jersey on days when it might be needed. Even on mild days rain can drop your core temperature rather quickly, and the jacket will earn its keep. Eyewear is a must. It protects the eyes from debris off the road or trail, rain, bugs, and other objects, not to mention the sun. For my eyewear and my helmet, I use products made by Rudy. My eyewear has lenses that are non-breakable and go from light to dark instantly as needed, and the helmet is one of the lightest and most protective helmets on the market. Finally, I wear Road ID tags and a bracelet. They both contain my medical info as well as emergency contact numbers and could save my life if I were to be rendered unconscious.

Everything else I may need is planned out before the journey and packed in my bags according to the conditions I will face. You need to fully understand the elements you will find yourself in before deciding on what you will pack and always err on the side of safety. In Chapter 8 I provide a complete list of what I carried on the Tour Divide verses what I carried on the Race Across Texas.

My normal kit consists of an Under Armour lightweight base layer tee, Bib shorts, Jersey, low cut Woolie Boolie socks, HR monitor strap, Rudy Helmet and glasses, Specialized skull cap, Pearl Izumi shoes with Showers Pass gloves and an Endura Pac a Jak stuffed in the back storage of the jersey.

Chapter 7

Every ounce counts — or does it?

The old saying "every ounce counts" is only somewhat true and can be a dangerous rule to follow. Less weight is certainly desirable as long as the attempt to lessen weight doesn't compromise safety. There are things we carry for survival, and there are things we carry for comfort and convenience; the rule applies to the latter only. When it comes to survival, weight is not an issue period. A friend of mine once made a statement to me while we were discussing the weight of the rain suit I was going to use on the Divide. He said that no one had every died from carrying too much weight in the wilderness, but many had died from hypothermia. I took the more robust rain suit, and it was the best choice I ever made. When it comes to things you need to survive unforeseen events that you have no control over, weight is not a deciding factor in the equipment you choose. **Staying dry and warm, staying hydrated, and knowing where you are should take precedence over everything else**. In the mountains as well as the deserts storms develop in a matter of minutes and can last for a matter of days, so be prepared.

The same goes for your bike and the way you set it up. The way you set up your wheels and the tires you use, for example, is an area that offers a lot of options for saving weight.

Less tape, lighter side-walled tires, and carbon wheels can all save you on overall weight, but when it's thirty-three degrees and raining with the wind howling on a muddy road at two in the morning in the wilderness, repairing a flat is the last thing you'll want to be doing. Before every race someone will inevitably ask me how much my bike weighs fully loaded, and my response is always the same: **whatever it needs to.**

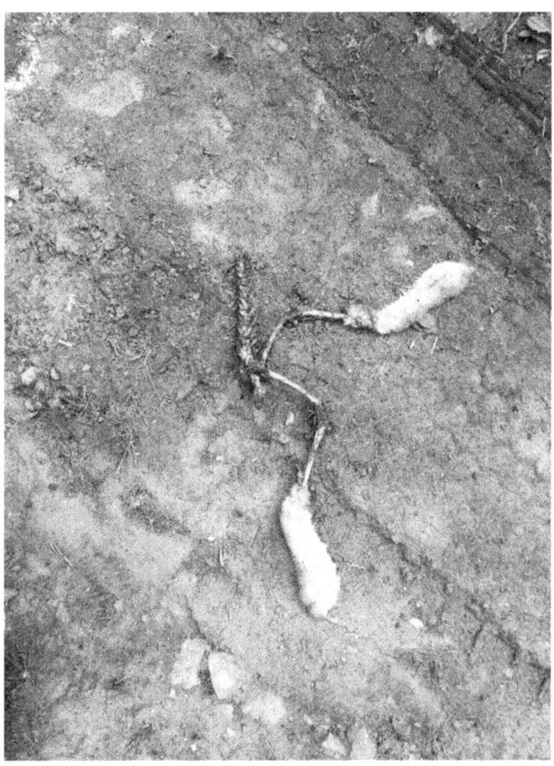

Chapter 8

What you really need

What we need to survive is never chosen by cost or weight but by quality and effectiveness. Materials needed to stay warm and dry include not only your clothes but also your shelter and sleeping materials. Always carry a water filtration system; you may be surprised as to where your water may have to come from. Multiple navigation devices and downloaded maps should always be available as well.

After returning from my adventures I always unpack my bike, and while doing so I question why I took certain items, then I smile and remind myself that I returned. When choosing the things I feel I need to survive, I spare no expense, and I never let weight become the deciding factor. Staying dry and warm, for example, is first on my list. I use a Showers Pass rain suit complete with waterproof socks and gloves. I didn't choose their lightest rain suit; I chose their most effective rain suit, the Refuge, for serious wilderness rides like the Divide. The suit is truly waterproof, as are their Crosspoint gloves and socks. Yes, they make a lighter suit (which I used on the Race across Texas), and yes, you can use plastic sacks wrapped around your feet to keep water out, and most of all, yes, you can die of hypothermia rather quickly. Showers Pass gear is the best I have ever found in doing what it says it will do, keep me dry and warm. My base layers come from Smart Wool; their products are made of the highest quality materials and perform exactly as stated. My sleeping bag is made by Montbell, and my tent by Big Agnes. Below is an example of how the gear you chose will differ depending on the conditions you will find yourself in.

The Tour Divide is a 3,000-mile race from Banff, Canada, to Mexico through some of the most remote country in North America. It consists of 200,000 feet of climbing, which would be like summiting Mt Everest 7 times. The route crosses the Continental Divide numerous times, and the terrain varies from mountains to deserts and everything in between. Much of the time there is limited cell service, and the weather conditions change in a moment's notice. Wildlife that you must share space with include grizzly bears, mountain lions, wolves, snakes, and such that can be unpredictable when it comes to their behavior. The race is a self-supported race, meaning you are responsible for you, your needs, as well as your safety.

Tour Divide setup

What I carried to stay dry and warm (stored in dry bags within seat bag)

- Rain suit (Refuge by Showers Pass)
- Waterproof gloves and socks by Showers Pass
- Arm warmers, leg warmers by Smart Wool, and Skyline cap by Showers Pass
- Base layer top and bottom by Smart Wool
- Socks by Defeet (Woolie Boolie)
- Warm Gloves by Showers Pass
- Down Hoodie by Montbell

What I carried for shelter and sleep (stored in dry bags within Handlebar roll)

- Big Agnes one-person Tent
- Montbell (Down Hugger 900) 40-degree sleeping bag
- Inertia Ozone KYLMIT sleeping pad
- Mylar emergency blanket by Global
- Pair of UA gym shorts and t-shirt
- Pair of skins compression tights
- Bic lighter
- Box of waterproof matches

What I carried to stay hydrated (stored on bike and in top right pocket of frame bag)

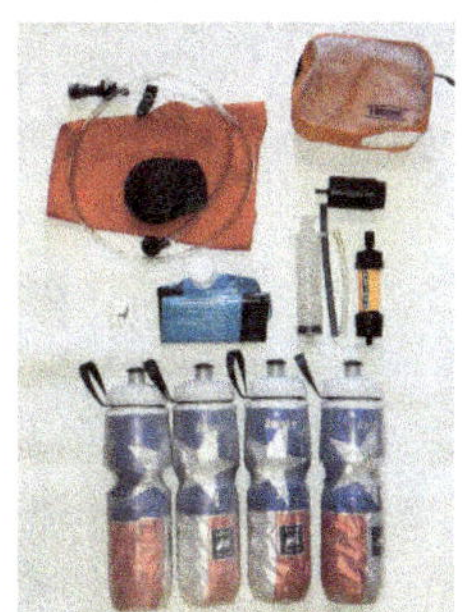

- 4 (24-ounce) insulated bottles and 1 (20-ounce) non-insulated bottle
- 1 (4-liter) bladder
- 1 Sawyer water filter with adaptable Berkey SPTrep filter for metals and pesticides
- Water tablets

What I carried for medical supplies (stored in top right pocket of frame Bag)

- Small tube triple antibiotic crème
- Small assortment of Benadryl, Tylenol, Bayer aspirin
- Daily meds packaged individual for each day
- Assortment of Band-Aids, gauze, and medical tape
- Allergy nose spray
- Several strips of KT tape and adhesive
- List of all meds taken daily and doses
- Small Bible, Razor
- Antibiotics – viral, and bacterial
- Several sting and bite pads
- Breathe Right strips
- Couple packs of Deep Blue pain rub

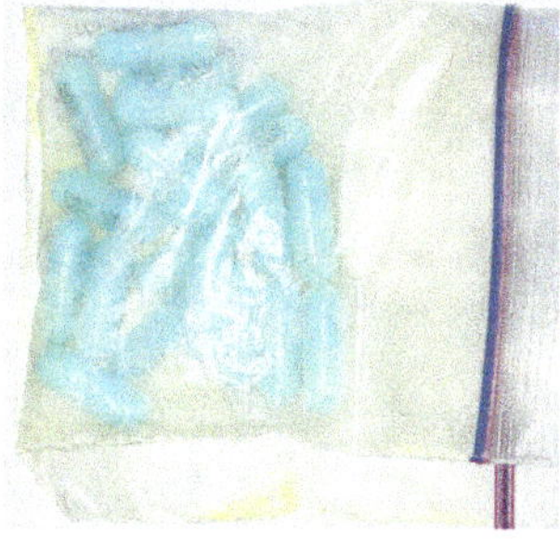

What I carried for hygiene (stored in jerrycan bag on top tube)

- Small roll degradable toilet tissue
- Compact toothbrush
- Small toothpaste
- Allergy eye drops
- Small tube of Carmex
- Fingernail clippers, Q tips
- Coleman Camp soap and towels
- Small tube of Gold Bond lotion
- Small tube filled with Bengay
- Couple Breathe Right strips
- $25
- Extra Bic lighter for fires (because it fit)

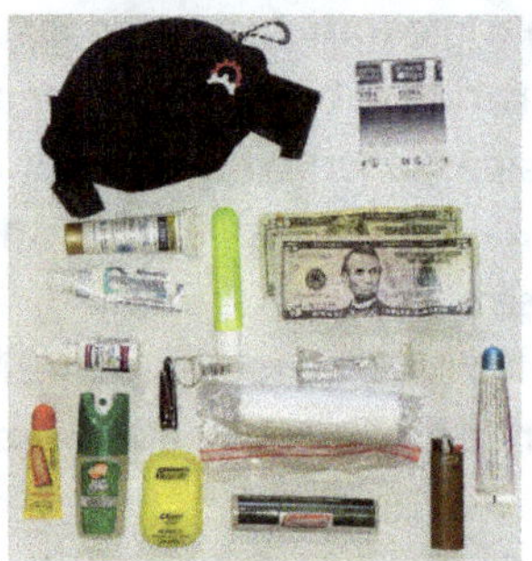

What I carried for safety (stored in top right pocket of frame Bag)

- Bear spray
- Bear whistle
- Bell mounted to bike
- Small J-frame Smith and Wesson 5-shot 357

What I carried for communication, navigation, and lighting (top left pocket of frame bag)

- 2 Garmin 1000 GPS units, both loaded with the routes
- Apple iPhone with pictures of the queue sheets and waypoints
- Spot Gen 3 tracking device
- Garmin Fenix Watch
- Maps of the route from Adventure Cycling
- Garmin handlebar camera
- K-Lite lighting system
- Aye-Up light and battery
- 4 Stix USB LED lights and mounts for helmet and camp
- Super Flash rear warning LED
- 2 Jockery stick batteries
- Lime fuel pass-through battery
- Extra phone and Garmin charging cables
- 1 multi USB charger block

What I carried for bike repair (stored in bottom right pocket of frame Bag)

Bag 1

- 2 inner tubes
- 1 Park Tool VP-1 patch kit
- 1 Park Tool GP-2 patch kit
- 2 Park Tool TB -2 tire boots
- 2 (25g) CO_2 cartridges and nozzle
- 1 (4-ounce) bottle orange seal
- 1 Lezyne handpump
- 1 valve stem
- 1 valve stem remover
- 1 heavy-duty tire tool

Bag 2

- Skeletool
- 1 (4-ounce) bottle Rock n Roll Extreme chain lube
- 1 small tube Tenacious tape
- 1 Kevlar spoke replacement
- 1 spare brake and 1 spare gear cable
- 1 chain brush
- 1 (12" x 12") chain rag
- Spare set of shoe cleats
- Spare derailleur hanger and screw
- 2 spare chain master links
- 1 Crankbrothers multi tool
- 1 golf tee wrapped with about 2 feet of monster tape
- Several cable ties and 2 small bungies
- 2 spare sets of brake pads

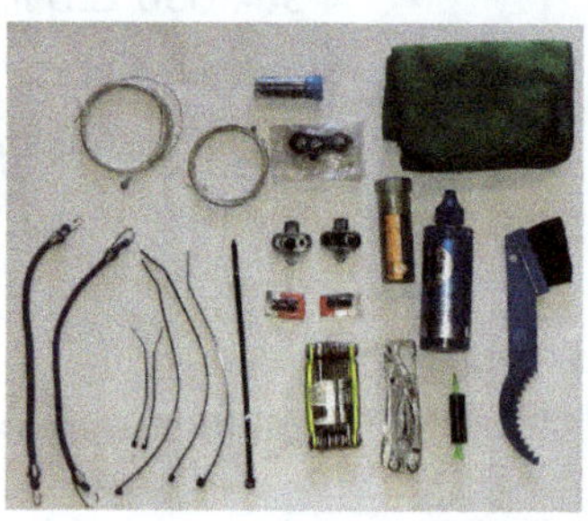

What I carried for music and money and comfort (stored in top left frame Bag)

- Small wallet with driver's license and handgun license copies, insurance card
- Credit card with small limit and $500 cash
- Small tube of Butt Paste, Desitin, and benzoyl peroxide
- Small iPod, Trekz Air, and readers
- Small cable and key lock

 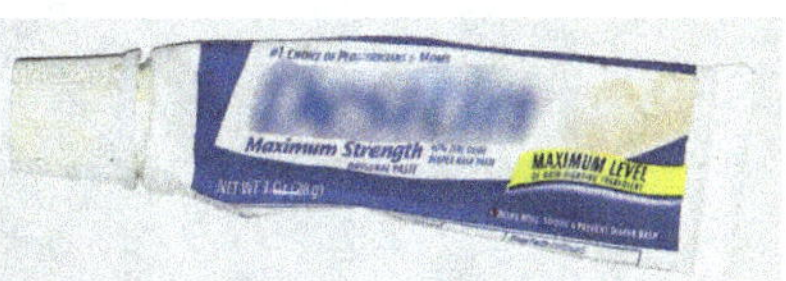

What I carried for nutrition (stored in handlebar bag)

- 1 (4-ounce) jar of honey
- 1 bottle Gu electrolyte capsules
- 3 packets Gu recovery drink mix for emergencies
- 5 Gu Stroopwaffles
- Bear bag
- Lightweight Backpack

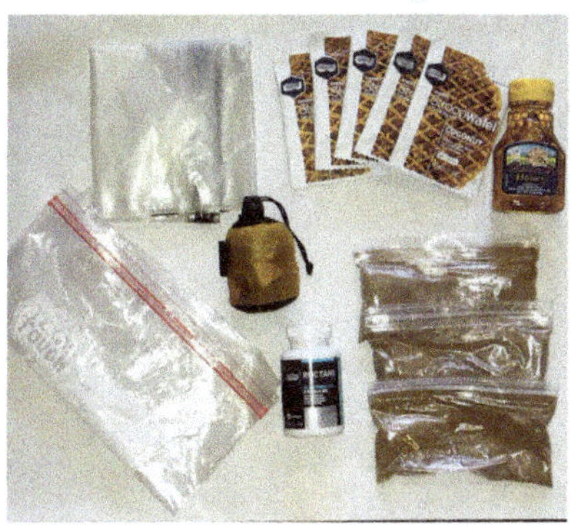

The Race Across Texas is a 1,029-mile race with mild terrain and a town always within 65 miles of wherever you are. I chose a belt-driven single-speed to race across Texas, and I chose to do it in June. The weather could get wet but not cold. Fighting heat requires a lot less supplies than does cold. Wildlife is pretty much limited to wild boar, wolves, bobcats, and snakes.

Race Across Texas setup

What I carried to stay dry and warm (stored in dry bags within seat bag)

- Rain suit (Elite by Showers Pass)
- Waterproof gloves
- Arm warmers, leg warmers, and Showers Pass cold weather cap
- Socks by Defeet (Woolie Boolie)
- Pair of UA gym shorts and t-shirt

What I carried for shelter and sleep (stored in dry bags within handlebar roll)

- Small emergency Bivey
- Mylar emergency blanket by Global
- 2 Bic lighters
- Box of waterproof matches

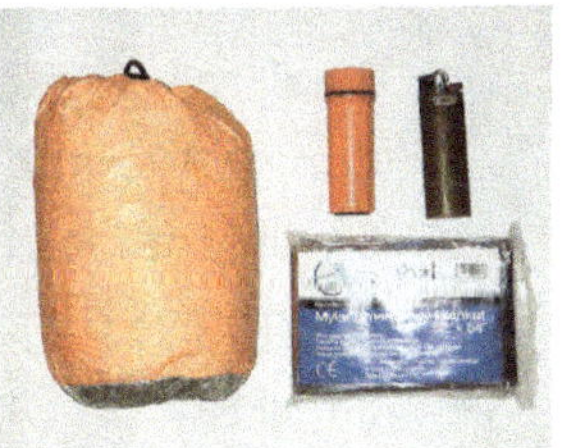

What I carried to stay hydrated (stored on bike and in top right pocket of frame bag)

- 4 (24-ounce) insulated bottles
- 1 (4-liter) bladder
- 1 Sawyer water filter / adaptable Berkey SPTREP filter for metals and pesticides
- Water tablets

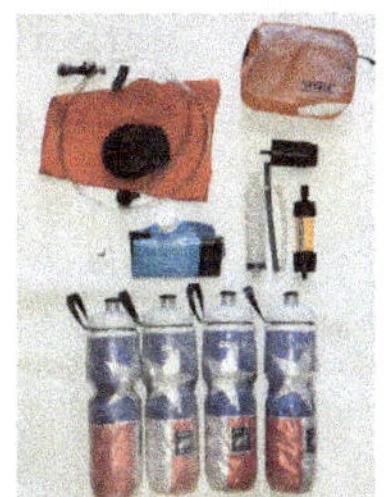

What I carried for medical supplies (stored in top right pocket of frame Bag)

- Small tube triple antibiotic crème
- Small assortment of Benadryl, Tylenol, Bayer aspirin
- Daily meds packaged individual for each day
- Assortment of Band-Aids, gauze, and medical tape, and a Razor
- Allergy nose spray
- Several strips of kt tape and adhesive
- List of all meds taken daily and doses
- Small Bible
- Several sting and bite pads
- Breathe Right strips
- Couple packs of Deep Blue pain rub

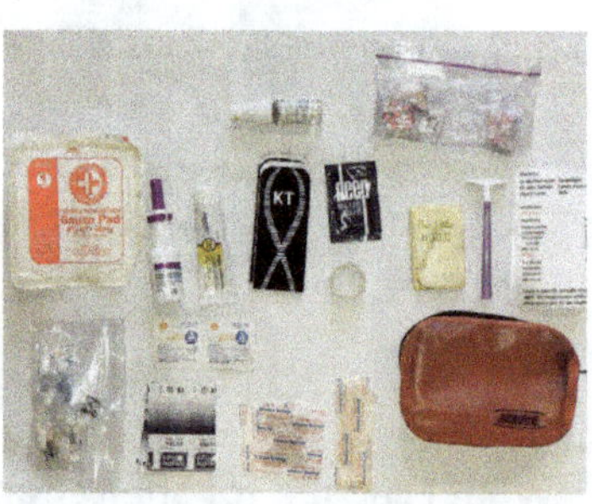

What I carried for hygiene (stored in jerrycan Bag on top tube)

- Small roll degradable toilet tissue
- Compact toothbrush
- Small toothpaste
- Allergy eye drops
- Small tube of Carmex
- Fingernail clippers
- Q tips
- Small tube of Gold Bond lotion
- Small tube filled with Bengay
- Couple Breathe Right strips
- $25
- Extra Bic lighter for fires (because it fit)

What I carried for safety (stored in top right pocket of frame bag)

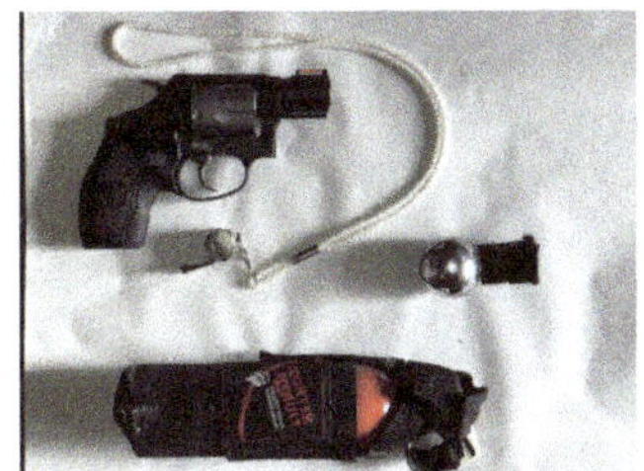

- Bear whistle
- Bell mounted to bike
- Small J-frame Smith and Wesson 5-shot 357

What I carried for communication, navigation, and lighting (top left pocket of frame bag)

- 2 Garmin 1030 GPS units, both loaded with the routes
- Apple iPhone with pictures of the queue sheets and waypoints
- Spot Gen 3 tracking device
- Garmin Fenix Watch
- Garmin handlebar camera
- K-Lite lighting system
- Aye-Up light and battery
- 4 Stix USB LED lights and mounts for helmet and camp
- Super Flash rear warning LED
- 2 Jockery stick batteries
- Lime fuel pass-through battery
- Extra phone and Garmin charging cables
- 1 multi USB charger block

What I carried for bike repair (stored in bottom right pocket of frame Bag)

Bag 1

- 2 inner tubes
- 1 Park Tool VP-1 Patch kit
- 1 Park Tool GP-2 patch kit
- 2 Park Tool TB -2 tire boot
- 2 (25g) Co2 cartridges and nozzle
- 1 (4-ounce) bottle orange seal
- 1 Lezyne handpump
- 1 valve stem
- 1 valve stem remover
- 1 heavy-duty tire tool

Bag 2

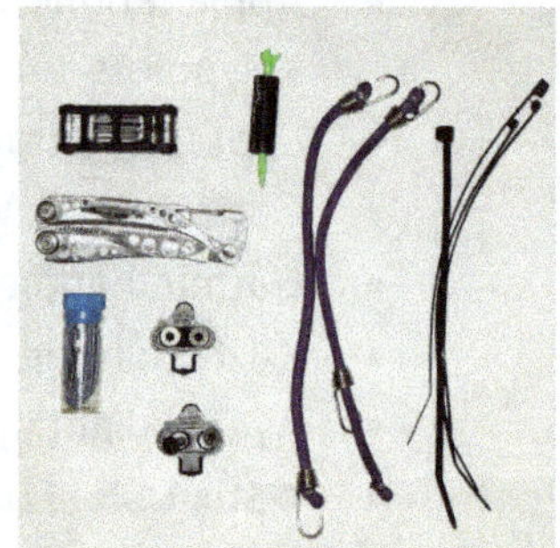

- Skeletool
- 1 Kevlar spoke replacement
- Spare set of shoe cleats
- 1 golf tee wrapped with about two feet
- monster tape
- Specialized S Work multi tool
- Several cable ties and 2 small bungies
- 2 sets of brake pads

Notice how small the tool kit, (bag 2) got when I switched from a chain to a belt ☺

What I carried for music and money and comfort (stored in top left frame bag)

- Small wallet with a driver's license and handgun license copies
- Credit card with small limit and $500 cash
- Small tube of Butt Paste, Desitin, and benzoyl peroxide
- Small iPod, Trekz Air Bluetooth headphones, and readers
- Small cable and key lock

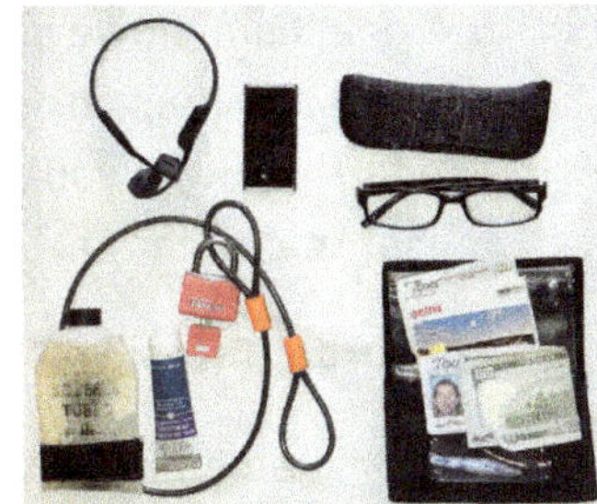

What I carried for nutrition (stored in handlebar bag)

- 1 bottle Gu electrolyte capsules
- 3 packets Gu recovery drink mix for emergencies
- 5 Gu Stroopwaffles
- Lightweight Backpack

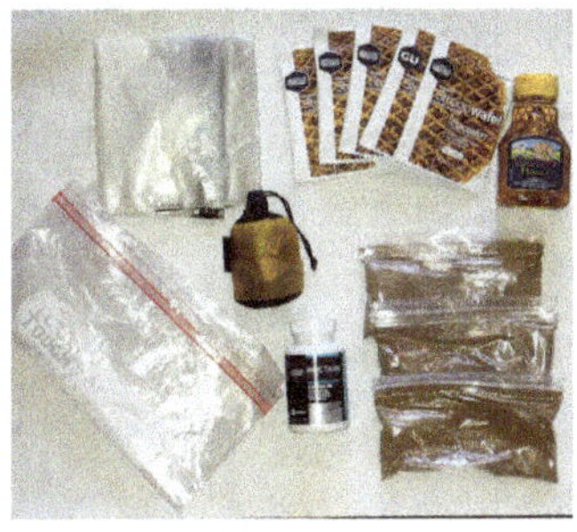

After a bit of trial and era you to will find what works best for you. **Remember, safety before weight.** Some of the supplies I carry for safety don't always set well with others. For example, I carry a small firearm (Smith & Wesson 357 J-frame 5-shot revolver) and have for 40 years. I have never once come remotely close to using it, and just like the emergency button on my SPOT Tracking device, I hope it stays that way. The firearm is not for animals but for those in the middle of nowhere who think you are easy prey on a Friday or Saturday night just off some old backroad. In the wilderness I feel much safer than I do when racing some of the backroads I've raced that scurry in and out of civilization. It is rare, but I have had cars with people shouting less than admirable things follow me into the country—so far, nothing more than throwing food or beverages. The world we live in is not was it used to be. That's sad but true. I am by no means advocating that you carry a firearm. No one should unless they are licensed and trained to use one. I am, however, saying be alert and pay attention to what's happening around you when camping near civilization. The farther away you are from populated areas, the better it is for setting up camp.

*****Border Crossings*****

Remember if your adventure takes you from one country to the next you will have to deal with border security and when doing so there are a couple of things you need to be aware of. Number one you will most likely need a passport and number two most countries take issue with one bringing drugs or weapons into their country. If a passport is required, make sure you take care of it long before your journey. You can get a passport at your local post office. The time frame given is 4-6 weeks from the time you submit your application, but I have seen it take up to 12 weeks to acquire, start the process early.

It is illegal to carry many weapons, especially a firearm across a border without a permit and a permit is not easy to get. Make sure you contact the country first and find out their rules before attempting to do so. Never be dishonest about what you are carrying, or your journey may include an extended stay that you were not planning on☺

In many cases it's a huge problem getting prescription drugs across the border as well. When I did the Tour Divide, I put each of my daily meds in small 1"x 1" bags labeled (morning and night) so all I had to do was take a bag at the appropriate time. I did not have to fumble with a lot of bottles, which take up a good bit of space on the bike. I also didn't have to worry about being able to read bottles or trying to remember which ones I had taken and which ones I hadn't. All in all, it made the process safer and easier for me. I did however take ever bottle label and place them on a zip lock baggy that I kept in my medicine kit. It's probably 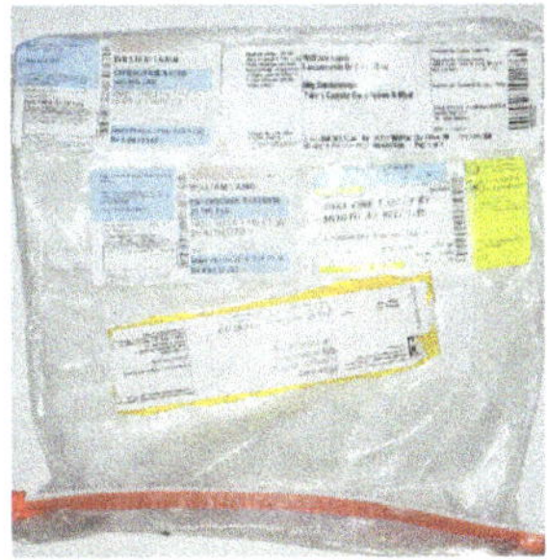 best to leave them in the original bottles if possible, they did however ok my passage.

Treat border agents with respect and they generally will do the same. Their job isn't as easy as it looks. When you enter another's country respect it and their policies as you would expect them to do if entering ours.

Chapter 9

What you carry for convenience and peace of mind

We all have things we take along that aren't necessary but make our trip more enjoyable, and after all, that's what it's all about. Items such as iPods, cameras, and certain sleep aids can make the experience more enjoyable, and the extra weight is miniscule. Phones now have such good built-in cameras and music apps that one could easily make a case not to carry anything but a phone. Just remember the phone could be a lifesaver and needs to stay charged. Long videos and tons of pics can also eat up storage, and for that reason I still carry a mini iPod and a Garmin handlebar-mounted camera with SD card. A small flask with your favorite spirits for those beautiful nights by a fire, a favorite cap to wear when you're not wearing your helmet, a lightweight pair of shoes or flip-flops for walking around the camp—yeah, a little more weight but well worth it. Small spirit stoves to heat water for coffee and pre-packed meals definitely add weight but also add to your enjoyment. There are several other items that can easily be added to this list; the important thing, however, is to understand these are conveniences and not necessities.

The old saying **"we pack our fears"** is most definitely true. The more knowledge you have however the less fear you have. Certain things that provide peace of mind like extra battery sticks, more clothing, and protection devices are also okay to carry. I have a friend who insists on carrying an extra tire casing in case he ruins a tire. Here are a couple of things to be considered when carrying the things that offer you peace of mind:

- A piece of duct tape rolled around a golf tee can serve as an excellent tire boot when a tire is cut and weighs very little, a lot less than a tire casing. ☺
- Animal deterrents such as bear spray need to be something you've practiced with and completely understand how to use, or you should not carry them; otherwise, you may render yourself disabled as opposed to the animal.
- You should never carry a firearm unless you are well versed in how to use one and unless you have an actual license to carry one. If you do have a license, it should be with you.
- Weight does become a factor when we are talking about things we don't need to survive. There are areas where you may have to push or carry your bike.

The farther I got along the route when doing the Tour Divide in 2016, the more equipment I found along the trail. Things that were really important to someone became less important as time went by—backpacks, sleeping bags, all sorts of things, especially clothing. Some of the items were valuable enough that I lugged them to the next town and shipped them home. The bottom line is to put some real thought into the extra things you carry. If they make you feel safer and cause you to worry less, pack them. Weight is weight and pushing or carrying the bike will remind you of that each time you have to do so. After several trips you will quickly sort out what you really need and what you are willing to carry anyway.

Chapter 10

Equipment: Do it right the first time

Everything is about money to some extent, and purchasing equipment is no different. When it comes to acquiring your equipment, do it right the first time. Don't settle for something that is close to what you decided you needed. If money is a big issue, there are some good used pieces available; you may just need to do a little homework before buying them. If it comes from the "what you really need gear," buy new only. Items such as sleeping bags and down hoodies tend to lose their effectiveness the older they are and if they are not cared for properly. Items that come from the "what you carry for peace of mind and comfort" list you can buy used and save. Items such as titanium handlebars and seat posts when bought used can save you money and perhaps even a one-man tent that you can pick up from someone who bought it and after using it a time or two decided it just wasn't for them.

Buying used bike frames when they are steel or titanium work well, but I would be careful buying carbon. As far as used complete bikes, there are some good deals out there, but you need to have a skilled and qualified mechanic check it out completely and then do several dry runs before your first outing. Even if you build your bike from scratch you should load it as it will be loaded during your event and ride it for several weeks to work out all the kinks before using it for an extended adventure.

I recommend loading and unloading your bike many times before you use it for several reasons:

- It helps you become very comfortable in knowing where everything is and how long it will take you to set up and take down while camping.
- It helps you determine exactly where things are best stored, making frequently used items more readily available.
- It helps you develop confidence that you've chosen the right equipment.

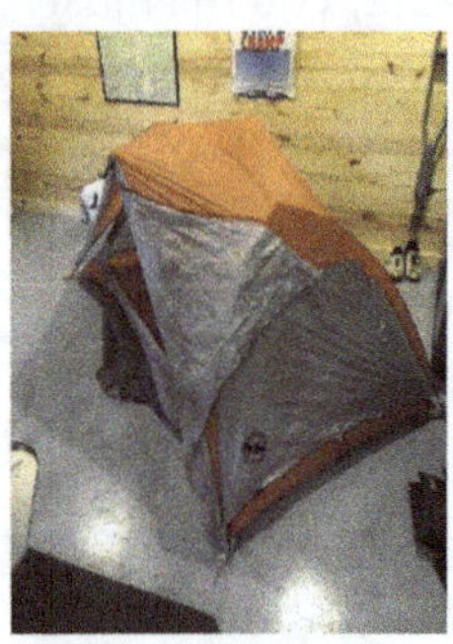

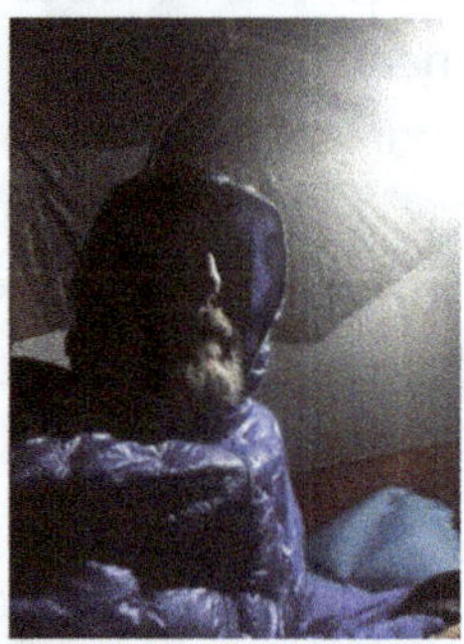

Chapter 11

Preparing for an adventure: The do's and don'ts

The Tour Divide in 2016 taught me a lot about how to prepare for an adventure. I had planned for a couple years as to how I was going to successfully navigate the Divide in eighteen days—everything from how far I would travel each day to exactly where I would bed down each night. I knew what I would eat and when. I knew where my supplies were coming from, had the route memorized, the places of interest, even the weather patterns for that time of year as well as the predictions for the year I had chosen. Every detail meticulously laid out. One day into the race erased 90% of my plans and within a few days it was a true adventure with complete unknown every step of the way.

Could I have planned better? Yes, but I had to make the mistakes first to know what I should have done differently. One must first understand that it is an adventure, meaning it will have unknowns. The key is to have a good understanding of what those unknowns could be and how you can prepare yourself for them. Things like weather predictions are not reliable; it's hard to predict how one will be able to navigate never-seen terrain. How far you will travel each day is not just dependent on how well you trained but also on adverse conditions you never expected. Storms, strong winds, loose sandy conditions, bike problems, spills, and several other variables can greatly reduce how far you travel in a day. Traveling shorter distances makes it farther to your next supply stop, for example, assuming that supply stop is still there. Several places I had read about in blogs that I depended on for supplies were no longer open, only open certain days of the week, or they closed early and opened late. This meant that if you got there after they closed you had to camp and wait until they opened the next day before you could get supplies and head to your next destination, which normally meant you just added a day to your total and everything forward had to be adjusted. Each mistake requires a new set of plans and doing so when you have limited phone service and access to the internet, at best becomes a choir and at worst a disaster.

There is no such thing as being overly prepared. Take the time to really access the elements in which you may find yourself and carry gear accordingly. Familiarize yourself with the route. Make an accurate list of towns and waypoints with exact distances between each one. After a long day on the bike, one mile can seem like twenty. Store phone numbers of emergency agencies along the way in a place where they are readily available. Always use a tracking device like SPOT that has an emergency search and rescue button on it. Never leave a destination without enough emergency rations to last you twice as long as you have allotted to get to your next destination. Being off the grid doesn't mean being stupid; always carry a phone even if you leave it off. At least it's available if you need it. Below is a list of some of the do's and don'ts when planning an adventure. Never, ever let your pride allow you to do something that you know is simply not worth the risk. Be aware of the wildlife around you. You are in their home; act accordingly. Understand beforehand that you're on an adventure and that facing unknowns is a certainty. Take deep breaths, take pictures, and most of all take time to fully embrace and enjoy the journey.

Do's

- Do verify supply stops and hours of operation by personally contacting each one beforehand.
- Do verify alternate routes in areas that are questionable.
- Do expect the unexpected. If it's predicted to be hot, be prepared for cold.
- Do take a first aid kit and be familiar with how to use everything in it.
- Do take a tracking device such as SPOT, regardless of the length or distance of the ride.
- Do send a share page from Spot or whatever app you are using to family and friends.
- Do underestimate your abilities and be pleasantly surprised.
- Do allow more time than needed.
- Do take pictures of maps and important info and store on your phone.
- Do keep riding if it is cold and raining, if possible.
- Do use bear bags to store your food when in the wild.
- Do make a list of towns and the distances between each one, as well as amenities there.
- Do take your phone.
- Do take a class in bike repair and practice what you learn.
- Do carry extra charging cords for your devices.

Don'ts

- Don't take anything for granted.
- Don't underestimate nature's fury.
- Don't depend on technology; it fails often.
- Don't eat things in nature unless you have great experience in doing so.
- Don't set daily goals based on your best efforts.
- Don't rely on anyone or anything other than the person in charge for information.
- Don't leave your cell phone at home.
- Don't stop in cold, rainy weather to camp, if possible.
- Don't approach wild animals to obtain pictures.
- Don't leave trash behind; take out what you took in.
- Don't wear headphones other than Trekz Air, these do not cover the ear canal and allow one to hear what's going on around them while still listening to music and weather by using bone technology, even then keep the volume low

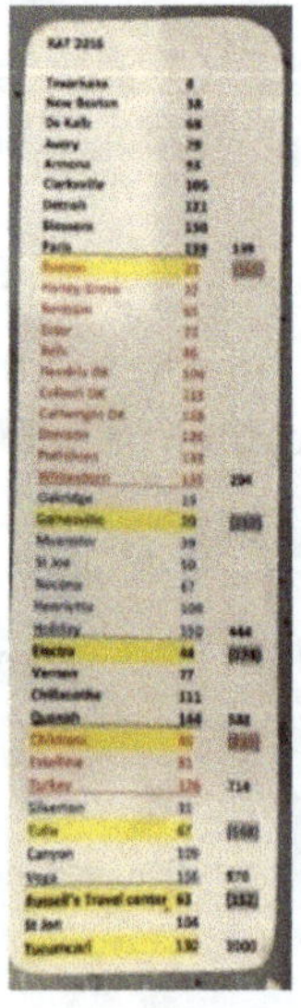

Chapter 12

Keeping a journal

Keeping a journal is one of the most rewarding things you can do. So much happens each day on our adventures that sometimes we misplace some special moments that may not seem special at the time. It's awesome to look back and see how things developed and how you dealt with them "at the moment" as well as the overall role they wound up playing in the journey.

Taking the time each night to reflect on the events of the day is a habit that should be adopted by all. Doing so can be extremely beneficial in several ways. It always helped me to unwind and, most importantly, allowed me to put down what I was feeling at that moment on paper. Many times, the next day was influenced by those words I'd scribbled down before sleep took me away. I wanted to remember everything, the good and the bad, long after the journey was over, and those scribblings had the ability to make it possible. It also helped me to recognize obvious mistakes I made and how I could have avoided them. Like a picture, words can have a dramatic effect, and years later they can take you back to a place and time in just a sentence or two. Journals can be kept using a small pad and pencil, a voice recorder, or even a cell phone. I write because perhaps someday my grandson will retrace some of my journeys and reading what I had to say about each day may be beneficial to him, but the choice is yours. Below is a short story about one of my races in 2014 from my book, *From There to Here.* The notes from my journal helped me to more accurately recall the events.

Race Across Texas 2014

As I look back, I believe the change I speak of began with the Race Across Texas in 2014. This was the first real adventure on a bike for me. When I first signed up for the Race I really had no idea what I was getting myself into. A race from Texarkana, Arkansas, to Tucumcari, New Mexico, about 1,000 miles of mostly trail, didn't sound too tough. Two and a half years ago I had quit playing golf, which is what I had done for a living over the last 25 years and stated riding mountain bikes. During those 2 ½ years I had raced pretty much every TMBRA series race that was held. I had also raced other races, such as The Whiskey 50, Leadville 100, and 24 Hours of Ole Pueblo. However, never had I raced multiple days in a row, especially when those days were to be 100-plus miles per day. The longest I had ever been on a bike at one time was 230 miles in a 24-hour race with support and on a bike that weighed about 21 lbs. A couple of weeks before the RAT I raced the Camino 205, which is an awesome race, and so I figured not only was I ready but that I was probably the favorite to win. ☺ Funny thing about getting older—the brain seems to frequently forget that its job is to think logically!

My friend Dave drove me to Texarkana the day before the race was to start. He also drove me the first 3 miles of the race leaving town to help me get familiar with the start and make sure my brand-new Garmin Oregon 650T was working properly. Dave, well, he's another story for another time. After getting everything laid out, I rested until the racers' meeting at 8. The meeting was a bit of an eye opener. We discussed the dangers of the race, like starting the same morning that deer

*season opened, and the condition of some of the trails,
treacherous at night for sure. After listening to the pitfalls as
well as everyone's experience levels, I went from thinking I was
the favorite to hoping I could finish and not become some
drunken hunter's hood ornament along the way!*

*The night's sleep was exactly like it always is before a
big race—nonexistent—and morning came too quickly. I ate my
pre-determined breakfast, got dressed, lined up for what I
thought was going to be a big deal... the start. Kevin said good
luck, and everyone took their time in just rolling out, didn't seem
like any race I'd ever been in. I was able to stay among the front-
runners for a long time, and then something I didn't expect to
happen happened—my Garmin froze. I stopped and tried to fix it
but with no luck. Riders were passing me, and by the time I got
back on the road I found myself in the place one doesn't want to
be without a working GPS unit, far enough behind the leaders
that I couldn't see them and far enough in front of the riders
having fun that I couldn't see them either. Much like in life, I was
alone, and the only help I had was me.*

*I followed bike tracks to a town called New Boston. No
tracks on pavement, but as fate would have it I saw a couple
riders at a DQ and pulled in. I worked feverishly on my Garmin
and got it working, I thought. After ordering something to eat I
gathered myself and formulated a plan. Originally, I was going
to say hi to my sis who worked in New Boston but had to scrap
that idea. I'd simply stay with these guys until the end of the first
segment to make sure my GPS was good, and at the check-in I
would get out my cue sheets, which I thought I'd never use, and
familiarize myself with the next part of the route. I knew at that
point I would have to be on my own since I wasn't stopping for
the night at that first checkpoint. Two of my grandkids live in
Blossom, but they were not in town that day so there was no
reason to tarry. Besides, I couldn't finish in 6 days unless I
covered the first 3 segments in two days. Also, I had lived in*

Paris, a town which the route would pass closely to, and still had an uncle who lived there that I wanted to see.

Along the next 70 miles to Blossom, which served as the end of our first segment, the Garmin froze several times, so I wasn't simply enjoying the ride like I thought I would but found myself worrying about things which I had no control over...pretty much like my everyday life. The route went through the south portion of Paris down Jefferson Road and then cut over to Washington. Jefferson Road—that sounded so familiar. As I rolled along the route I passed the junior high school and remembered that as being the high school that I attended for half a year as a freshman. Then, as I turned on Jefferson Road, I found myself at an intersection looking right at an old, run-down house. It dawned on me that was the last place I lived with my dad. The route took me not only past the very house but back to a time in my life that I hadn't thought about in a long time.

As I stood over my bike and stared at the house it seemed like only yesterday, and yet it was 41 years ago. Barely 15 years of age, after a big fight with my dad, I ran out of that house and became an adult who had to support himself from that moment on. My whole life came rushing back. Overwhelmed with emotions, I just stood there. I could almost see a much younger me running out that door, scared yet relieved that it was over;. My prayers were answered, and now I was free. That younger me stopped and stared at the road as if he saw me there, and I couldn't help but think if I could only speak to him even for a moment what would I say. As he threw gravel leaving that driveway on his way to me, I pushed the pedal over and begin rolling away. Even though I couldn't speak to him, I felt he was speaking to me.

My aunt had just passed away about 3 months before the race. I promised many times to come see her, but life kept me too busy until the funeral of course. That's why I was going to stop and see my uncle while I was there. In just one moment I went from worrying about getting lost with my GPS acting up to realizing I had been navigating for a long time without one. A calm came over me as I rode through the streets of a town I had lived in for a short time but that had changed my life so dramatically. I turned the Garmin off and proceeded to my uncle's house on the north side of town. After a good visit, I headed for Roxton, Texas, where I would spend the first night of the race in a bed-and-breakfast with a fellow racer, Rick Pressor. The cue sheets were easy to read for that part of the segment, and the sunset led to a chilly night, but the end of that day's ride was sweet. We had the place to ourselves, and the owners were nice enough to leave us a chicken salad in the fridge. I ate, cleaned up, and went to bed.

I replaced the batteries in the Garmin a third time, and it was working. My focus got back on riding hard and finishing the second and third segments by the end of the day. Basically, a 170-mile day. We all had reason to press forward due to the forecast of some cold and wet stuff that was a definite. One section of the trail was iffy in good weather but would be virtually unpassable in bad. I really wanted to pass that point. After a good night's rest, I got an early start and headed to Arrowhead State Park. My legs felt surprisingly good, as did I… maybe I could win this race! It was probably my best day thus far on a bike. I felt good, the scenery was good, and my mind still hadn't come back to the reality of what we were doing. My trusty steed and I decided to keep going past Arrowhead State Park and into Wichita Falls for the night. I really wanted to beat the rain to Vernon. The next morning started well. The front had arrived but not in full force, and Vernon was in sight. As the day progressed, the worst became a reality. Wind, rain, and mud made the trail impossible to ride and not very easy to push, which is what I did for most of the day. One thing was for sure: whichever way I was going, it was always into the wind and uphill! I had found the Bermuda Triangle of Northwest Texas.

The trail was so bad, but there was no way to get off it. I couldn't just head up some makeshift gravel road because I had no idea where it would lead. Back to real life again, plans hardly ever work the way we want them too. I just did what I had done most of my life—I simply kept moving forward. If I died frozen, wet, and alone out here, so be it. I had made up my mind I was not going to let anything else bother me. It began raining harder, the winds got stronger, the mud thicker, and then came my first flat. I was only a bit pissed. After putting a tube in the rear tire of a bike that weighs 68lbs in mud with a tire that was clearly smaller than the wheel it was on one could probably gather I was a tad more pissed than before. I finally made it to a section that I could ride and found a country store to get food and warm up a bit. The elderly man behind the counter (I won't say old for obvious reasons) asked me a good question. He said, "Son, what the hell you doing on a bike in this kind of weather way out here?" I told him about the race, and his reply was, "If that don't beat all I ever seen." At that point, I pretty much agreed with him. ☺ I pressed on and decided to go all the way to Quanah to get a motel and clean up.

When I got up the next morning I realized that this was a bit more than I had anticipated, but physically I still felt great. The problem that arose was mental. I now was riding to finish, and suddenly I became aware of my Strada Cateye and the miles ticking by. For the first time I became restless and in a hurry to reach the next checkpoint. My bum had become sore for whatever reason, and I was using a towel that I found along the way to ease the pain. After a long climb out of the saddle the towel had fallen off, and I didn't want to go back after it, so I tried several things I came across like a piece of cardboard that I folded. Nothing worked. When I finally found a store in a town we passed through that had towels I bought one. It helped maybe, but the race had now become something I had to finish and no longer something I looked forward to doing. The change occurred without me knowing, much like it does in life. We go into things excited and with great plans, and somewhere along the way we get lost with all that is happening around us and forget the real reason we are where we are and can only focus on where we want to be next. My goal was to make Cap Rock Canyon by nightfall, but I was mentally spent and stopped in Turkey instead. I stayed in the old Turkey hotel. It was old and run-down, really kind of eerie. After I checked in, Mark Pruett and Rick Presser arrived. We all had dinner together along with a retired pilot who was staying there; it was nice just to talk to someone again. Only 2 days left, and I will have accomplished my goal!

Next morning, I headed off to Herford, the last checkpoint before Tucumcari. The day was pretty nice, but the miles ticked off so slowly. I felt like I would never finish and grew frustrated early. Then I formulated another plan. I could no longer think in terms of hundreds of miles to checkpoints; I had to break it down into small battles that kept my mind occupied. It became, "Okay, only 8 miles to Quitaque, then only 23 miles to Post Office, now only 35 miles to Kress," and so on. Before I knew it, I was in Herford by nightfall. Life lesson: just set small goals. It makes the big goals much more attainable. I felt the need to go on to Tucumcari that night while the wind was low. No different than any 24-hour race, it would hurt, but it was only 100 more miles. Dave called and informed me that according to the View Ranger tracking app we were using, all of us at the front were stopped in Herford, so I decided to get a good night's sleep and race tomorrow. The other guys were smarter than I and left about 4 a.m. I didn't leave till 6 a.m.—what a mistake. It turned out to be the toughest 100 miles I have ever ridden. The wind was furious at about 30 mph and there was not an object taller than a stick in any direction as far as one could see. At times I found myself moving at a pace of about 3 mph. Every time I stood to rest my back from leaning so far forward, my towel would blow off. I spent a good deal of time chasing that frickin' towel. Uphill into the wind, nothing could be worse except for the New Mexico welcome center, where I had planned on refueling, being on the opposite side of the interstate with huge fences between me and it. Worn out and tired, I simply again did what I do best—pressed on. By sunset I could see the lights of Tucumcari. What a beautiful sight! When I got to the finish line, Mark and Rick were there to welcome me. I had finished—and fifth at that.

*Lying in bed that night, it hit me like a ton of bricks. It was done! All the planning for months, the anticipation, the nerves, the not knowing what was to come, the adventure, it was over. Hate to say it, but it was emotional. I felt empty, not sure what I would do the next day. I then realized that the way I raced was much like the way I lived, in a rush. So many great memories of the last week came rushing back, even the hard times made me laugh. So many things, experiences, sights, and the beautiful awareness of being alive... I wished I could share it all with the ones I love. If it was so great, however, why the rush? Why was I in such a hurry to get **from there to here? It reminded me of life, the way many of us live our lives. Always in a hurry to finish something, to get somewhere. Always complaining about the big picture album and never looking at the pictures. You know what I learned? I learned that where we come from not only makes us who we are but that it's still there and should be visited from time to time to remind us of how we became who we are. I learned it's easier to eat a cake one slice at a time and that the taste lasts longer that way. I learned that to reach our destination we should sometimes drag our feet. God allowed us an adventure with a definite beginning and a definite end; the journey between those two points is what we make it. He thought enough of us to give it. The least we can do is take it and make it as great as we can.***

Roadrunner
LODGE

Chapter 13

What to Eat When Supplies are Hard to Come by

Let's face it, it is difficult to carry enough food for a multiple-day ride in the wilderness. When supplies are only available every couple of days we must be particular about what we eat and what we carry to the next stop. For me, this is a huge problem because I am a health nut and not fond of eating junk food. There are a couple of important things that are givens and must be fully understood:

- Fuel, in the form of food and water, are what keep your body functioning.
- Fuel comes in different forms, some being more beneficial than others.
- Some fuel sources work much slower than others.
- It takes a certain amount of fuel to keep your body functioning a certain amount of time.

Let me start by saying I am by no means a nutritional expert. What works for me may not work as well for you. But this chapter should give you a good idea of what you're facing when it comes to staying fueled during your journey.

The food you choose is of great importance for maintaining energy levels. Carbohydrates supply your body with energy in the form of glucose. Higher-quality carbs provide you with sustained energy, whereas low-quality carbs provide you with more of a quick burst of energy for a short period of time. You will need both. Carbohydrates are the body's preferred source of fuel, but protein also plays an important part in the fueling process. Protein is needed for repairing, maintaining, and growing muscle tissue. Also, during exercise, stored fat in the body is used as fuel. Fatty acids are transported through the blood to muscles, but the process is relatively slow compared to the process of turning carbohydrates into fuel. Eating a well-balanced diet is great but not always possible when supply stops are days apart and space on the bike is limited.

Many times, we must pack food in between stops that will last several days and not spoil. Knowing what to carry that gives you the most good for the space it occupies is a must. When reaching a destination where full meals are available, you should always take advantage and leave that stop fully fueled before heading to your next destination. Below is a list of readily available foods in all groups that you can pack easily between waypoints:

- **High-Quality Carbs:** Whole wheat bagels, dried fruits, carrots, celery, pizza, crackers, chips, bean dip
- **Low-Quality Carbs:** cookies from Subway, packaged pastries, gummy bears, 4 oz bottle of honey
- **Protein:** Packaged tuna, cheese sticks, beef jerky, trail mix, protein bars

Bagels covered with honey always serve as a good breakfast for me, and trail mix, subway cookies, and gummy bears are the perfect snacks throughout the day. Tuna lunchable's were a staple and easy to carry as were Pizza and beef Jerky.

A good rule of thumb is to drink every 15 minutes and to eat every 30 minutes throughout the day. When available, chocolate milk is a good recovery drink. I carry several pouches of GU Energy chocolate smoothie recovery drink mix for emergencies, as well as a few GU Stroopwaffles. Both are easy to pack and are of the highest quality.

I started the Tour Divide at 170 pounds and finished at 144. The weight loss was mostly due to my inexperience with supply stops and overall understanding of nutrition; it was a great learning experience. During the Race Across Texas a year and a half later, I lost 2 pounds and took in about 4,000 calories a day. Lesson learned.

There is another nutritional plan that has really taken off called *ketosis.* If you're healthy and eating a balanced diet, your body controls how much fat it burns, and you don't normally make or use ketones. But when you cut way back on your calories or carbs, your body will switch to ketosis for energy. Billy Rice, a coach and fitness guru in Texas, has had great success with it as have his students. The process focuses on using adipose tissue or fat for fuel and requires about six weeks of training. The body has enough adipose tissue available to fuel a person for an extended period requiring little if any outside food source. It's worth checking out. Billy's info is as follows: **Invictus Ultra-Distance Coaching on Facebook**

Chapter 14

Safety

As Jay Petervary says, **Safety is no accident**. Safety begins with a conscious thought. Before you get on a bike, whether its riding downtown or in the great outdoors, safety should be your first priority.

Let's start with streets, roads, and other areas that we share with automobiles. You as a cyclist have exactly the same rights as people in motor vehicles. **You also have the same responsibilities**. Always ride your bike as if you were driving a car; if it's illegal in a car, it's illegal on a bike period. Avoid riding east early mornings or west late afternoons if possible. Motorists will be looking directly into the sun, and that puts you in more danger. Always wear highly visible clothing and carry everything on your bike you need in case the weather takes a turn for the worst. Let someone know when you leave, where you are going, when you expect to return, and the route you will follow. This is easily done using apps such as Map My Ride. Wear a helmet; it's okay to be uncool and live.

Before biking in the wilderness, get to know what animals you'll be sharing space with, as well as their behaviors. Familiarize yourself with conditions that make storms likely; when possible, check weather forecasts; and be prepared by having the equipment necessary to shelter yourself from those storms. Make sure you carry enough supplies to get you to your next stop, especially water; you will not die from carrying an excess. Safety is just using a little common sense and knowing when to check your pride at the door. **A little fear is a good thing, to be somewhat afraid doesn't mean you are unwilling to do something, it just means you understand the dangers and that you respect them.**

As Matthew Crompton, an award-winning writer and photographer, says "you never know how much is enough until you also know how much is too much." It could not have been said better. It's part of our soul to be adventurous and seek the "too much" and when we find it we should embrace and more importantly respect it so that someday we may find it again:)

Chapter 15

Equipment recommendations

Adventuresbybike.com

Aftershokz.com (for Trekz Air headphones)

Baryak.com

Bikebagdude.com

Brooksengland.com

E-rudy.com

Gatescarbondrive.com

Guenergy.com

Invictus Ultra-Distance Coaching Facebook

Kliteusa.net

Laufcycling.com

Montbell.com

Revelatedesign.com

Salsacycles.com

Showerspass.com

Smartwool.com

Speedgearbike.com

Spotbrand.com

Teravail.com

"I return from every bike packing adventure with one regret, and that is that I can't share all that I felt and saw with the rest of the world. The lens of a camera captures but a still image, a moment in time, and yet that image can overwhelm when it's viewed upon by the human eye. The eye doesn't simply see, but it also allows the brain to imagine what it felt like to be in that moment. Simply put, a photograph doesn't come close to allowing the viewer to feel what it feels like to be a part of that moment." *–William R. Lamb*